Forestry

Tatiana Tomljanovic

Weigl

CALGARY

www.weigl.com

Published by Weigl Educational Publishers Limited
6325 10 Street S.E.
Calgary, Alberta T2H 2Z9

Library of Congress Cataloging-in-Publication Data

Tomljanovic, Tatiana
    Forestry / Tatiana Tomljanovic.
(Linking Canadian communities)
Includes index.
ISBN 978-1-55388-373-9 (bound)
ISBN 978-1-55388-374-6 (pbk.)
    1. Forests and forestry--Canada--Juvenile literature. 2. Forests and
forestry--Economic aspects--Canada--Juvenile literature. 3. Forests and
forestry--Canada--History--Juvenile literature. I. Title. II. Series.
SD145.T64 2007   j634.90971   C2007-902245-6

Printed in the United States of America
1 2 3 4 5 6 7 8 9 11 10 09 08 07

Editor
Heather C. Hudak
Design
Warren Clark

All of the Internet URLs given in the book were valid at the time of publication. However, due to the
dynamic nature of the Internet, some addresses may have changed, or sites may have ceased to exist
since publication. While the author and publisher regret any inconvenience this may cause readers,
no responsibility for any such changes can be accepted by either the author or the publisher.

Every reasonable effort has been made to trace ownership and to obtain permission to reprint copyright
material. The publishers would be pleased to have any errors or omissions brought to their attention so
that they may be corrected in subsequent printings.

We acknowledge the financial support of the Government of Canada through the Book Publishing
Industry Development Program (BPIDP) for our publishing activities.

Contents

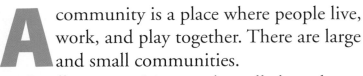
What is a Community?

A community is a place where people live, work, and play together. There are large and small communities.

Small communities are also called rural communities. These communities have fewer people and less traffic than large communities. There is plenty of open space.

Large communities are called towns or cities. These are urban communities. They have taller buildings and more cars, stores, and people than rural communities.

Canada has many types of communities. Some have forests for logging. Others have farms. There are also fishing, energy, **manufacturing**, and mining communities.

Types of Canadian Communities

FARMING COMMUNITIES
- use the land to grow crops, such as wheat, barley, canola, fruits, and vegetables
- some raise livestock, such as cattle, sheep, and pigs

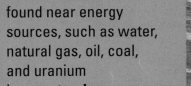

ENERGY COMMUNITIES
- found near energy sources, such as water, natural gas, oil, coal, and uranium
- have **natural resources**
- provide power for homes and businesses

FISHING COMMUNITIES
- found along Canada's 202,080 kilometres of coastline
- fishers catch fish, lobster, shrimp, and other underwater life

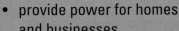

Real Canadian Communities

Yellowknife
Northwest Territories
mining community

Fort McMurray
Alberta
energy community

Powell River
British Columbia
**forestry
community**

Shaunavon
Saskatchewan
**farming
community**

Oshawa
Ontario
**manufacturing
community**

Terence Bay
Nova Scotia
**fishing
community**

FORESTRY COMMUNITIES
- found near forests
- loggers cut down trees for building supplies and making paper

MINING COMMUNITIES
- found in areas rich in **minerals**, such as zinc, nickel, and diamonds
- miners dig into the ground for minerals

MANUFACTURING COMMUNITIES
- use natural resources to make a finished product
- finished products include cars and computers

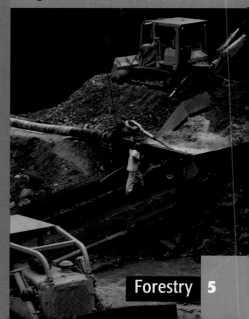

Welcome to a Forestry Community

Powell River is a forestry community in British Columbia. It is a small town near the Pacific Ocean. There are large forests on the land around Powell River.

Many of the people who live in Powell River work in the forestry industry. They also work in businesses that make forest products. Some people cut down trees. The logs are made into other goods, such as **lumber** and paper.

There is a pulp and paper mill in Powell River. In the mill, logs are made into paper goods. These are used to make items such as newspapers and books. There is also a sawmill in Powell River. Logs are cut into boards. They are for building houses and making furniture.

Special equipment is needed to cut down and move large logs.

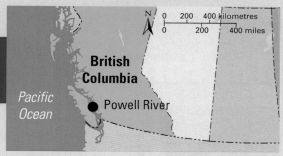

British Columbia

Pacific Ocean

Powell River

"My name is Julie. I like to play on the hills around Powell River. There are forests, too. Many of the trees are cut down. They are sent to the pulp and paper mill where my dad works. Some of our neighbours work there, too. My dad sends the wood pulp through the dryer. The paper that he makes is sent to many places.

Powell River is right next to the Pacific Ocean. In the summer, my family kayaks on the ocean. There are no big waves because the water near Powell River is protected from the wind. In winter, I like to walk to the skating rink with my brothers, David and Benjy. Every Saturday, I go shopping with my mom."

Think About It
Compare Powell River to your community.
- **How is it the same?**
- **How is it different?**

The Forestry Industry

Logging companies cut down, or log, trees. Other companies make wood and paper products. Together, they make up the forestry industry. This is an important industry for communities that are set in forested places.

The forestry industry provides many jobs for people in British Columbia. Some work in the forests logging. They make other wood and paper products. Products from the forestry industry are used in communities across Canada.

Trucks carry logs to sawmills.

Timeline

1600s

Trees from Canada are cut to supply **timber** for ships in France and Great Britain.

1800s

Canada supplies trees for the pulp and paper industry in France and Great Britain.

1900

The Canadian Forestry Association is formed. The association protects forests from being overused.

Most of Canada's forests have softwood trees. Pine, spruce, and fir are softwood trees. Softwoods are easy to work with. They are softer than hardwoods, such as birch and maple. Most softwood lumber is used for building houses and furniture.

Lumber is a "first-stage" wood product. This means that timber only goes through one step to become lumber. When trees are first cut down, the timber is sent to a sawmill. The logs are cut into boards called lumber. At this point, the lumber is ready to be sold.

Canada's forestry industry makes about $80 billion every year.

1926

Andreas Stihl invents a chainsaw. Before chainsaws, loggers used hand saws to cut down trees.

1949

The Canada Forestry Act is passed. It helps the forestry industry in Canada to grow.

1992

Canada starts its Model Forest Program to make sure people can enjoy Canada's forests in the future.

Pulp and Paper Mills

More than half of the trees cut down in Canada are made into wood pulp. When wood is cut into boards, smaller pieces are left over. These pieces are cut into wood chips. Steam and chemicals are added. This makes the chips into a thick "soup." The soup is wood pulp.

Wood pulp is used to make many paper products. Brown paper bags, cardboard boxes, newsprint, and toilet paper all come from wood pulp. Canada has more than 155 pulp and paper mills. They are found in rural areas, near forests.

In 2004, Canada made 26 million tonnes of wood pulp.

Pulp and Paper Mill Process

Loggers cut down trees.

Branches and bark are removed.

Logs are shipped to a sawmill.

Logs are cut into lumber.

Small pieces of wood are left over from the lumber. They are chopped into wood chips.

Steam and chemicals are used to break down wood chips into wood pulp.

The pulp is put through a dryer.

To make white paper, wood pulp is treated with more chemicals and **bleached** white.

A big machine winds the bleached pulp into paper.

The paper is shipped to customers.

Canadian Forests Map

This map shows some of Canada's forest areas. Canada has 310 million **hectares** of forest. Most of the forests can be used for logging. The other forests are in parks and on private land. They cannot be used for logging. Canadian companies cut down 0.4 percent of the forests that can be logged. Most of the wood is used to make lumber and paper.

Legend

- Taiga Cordillera
- Taiga Plains
- Boreal Cordillera
- Taiga Shield
- Boreal Plains
- Hudson Plains
- Boreal Shield

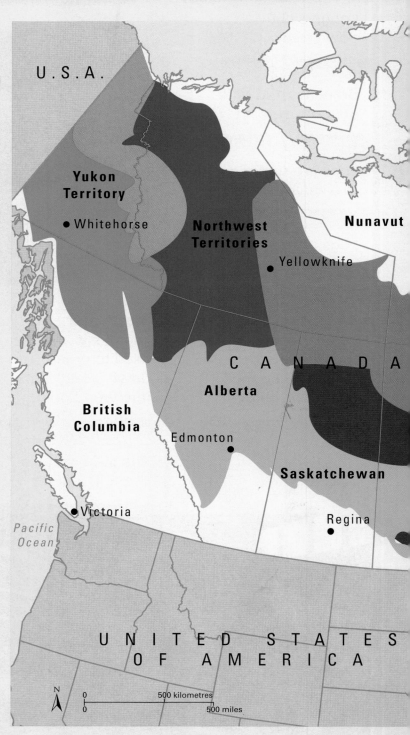

U.S.A.

Yukon Territory

• Whitehorse

Northwest Territories

Yellowknife

Nunavut

C A N A D A

Alberta

British Columbia

Edmonton

Saskatchewan

• Victoria

Regina

Pacific Ocean

U N I T E D   S T A T E S
O F   A M E R I C A

N

0   500 kilometres
0   500 miles

Iqaluit

Labrador Sea

Hudson Bay

Newfoundland
and Labrador

Manitoba

St.
John's

Quebec

Prince Edward
Island

Ontario

New
Brunswick

Charlottetown

Nova
Scotia

Winnipeg

Quebec
City

Fredericton

Halifax

Ottawa ★

Atlantic Ocean

Toronto

Careers

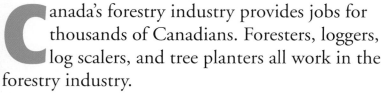

Canada's forestry industry provides jobs for thousands of Canadians. Foresters, loggers, log scalers, and tree planters all work in the forestry industry.

Foresters decide when, where, and how to log forests. They make sure forest wildlife, fish, and water are protected. Foresters make sure all logging activity is **legal** and safe.

Loggers also work in the forestry industry. They cut down trees. Then, log scalers inspect the logs. They weigh and measure the logs. After that, they assign a **grade**.

Foresters plan how to plant trees in places that have been logged. This helps grow new forests for future use.

Tree planters are hired to plant new trees. Tree planting happens at certain times of the year. In British Columbia, planting begins in February or March.

Many types of businesses support the forestry industry. They provide jobs, too. Some businesses ship Canada's lumber and paper products to customers. Others provide chemicals and packing materials for pulp and paper mills.

Sometimes, seedlings, or baby trees, are planted where trees have been logged.

Ships are used to transport, or move, lumber.

Think About It
What other jobs might there be in the forestry industry?

Links Between Communities

Everyone is part of a community. It may be a village, a town, or a city. Communities are linked to one another. Each Canadian community uses goods that link it to other communities. Goods are things people grow, make, or gather to use or sell.

A forestry community makes lumber for construction. The wood may be shipped to another community to build houses or furniture.

Energy communities produce natural gas, oil, and other types of energy, such as wind, solar, and hydro. Other communities use this energy to power their homes and vehicles.

Dairy products and meats come from farming communities that raise cattle and other animals. People in all communities drink milk products and eat meat from these communities. Many farming communities grow crops such as wheat. Wheat is used to make bread and pastries.

These goods may be fish, grains, cars, and paper products. Communities depend on one another for goods and services. A service is useful work that is done to meet the needs of others. People are linked when they use the goods and services provided by others.

Manufacturing communities make products such as cars and trucks. They also make airplanes, ships, and trains that are used to transport, or move, people and goods from one place to another. Transportation services help communities build links.

Fishing communities send fish to stores to be bought by people in other places. In Canada, most fish is caught off the Pacific or Atlantic coast. People living on farms or in cities across the country buy the fish at stores.

Diamonds, gold, and potash can be mined. These items are sent from mining communities to other parts of the country. A diamond might be set in a ring for a person in another community.

Think About It
In your community, what goods and services help meet your family's needs and wants?

The Environment

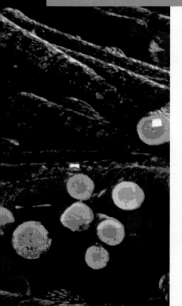

More than half of the wood cut in Canada is logged in British Columbia. Many trees are logged to make goods for Canadian communities and communities around the world.

Logging can damage the environment. Trees make much of the **oxygen** that people and animals breathe. They are homes for animals. Trees also keep the soil in place with their roots. When a forest is logged, the animals that live there lose their homes. Without tree roots to hold it in place, the land may slide or blow away.

More than half of the wood cut in Canada is logged in British Columbia.

Think About It

Each tree takes 70 to 80 years to grow big enough to be logged. How can we be sure that people in the future will be able to have books made of paper from trees?

Chemicals are used to make wood pulp. They are released into the air and water. Some of these chemicals can harm the environment.

People need wood and paper products. They must also care for the forests. Scientists are helping to replace trees that have been cut down. They have made new types of trees that grow quickly. Tree planters plant the new types of trees so forests can grow faster.

Eco-friendly Pulp and Paper Mill Process

People who work at pulp and paper mills are finding better ways of working. Researchers and scientists are helping mills do less damage to the environment.

Yonghao Ni is a researcher. He studies and finds ways to improve paper production. Yonghao found a way of bleaching paper that uses less **peroxide**. Yonghao called this new bleaching method the PM process. The PM process is used in mills across North America.

Brain Teasers

Test your knowledge by trying to answer these brain teasers.

Q *What type of community is Powell River?*

A Powell River is a forestry community.

Q *What work do log scalers do?*

A Log scalers weigh and measure logs. They also grade the logs.

Q *What goods might a forestry community make?*

A Forestry communities make lumber or paper.

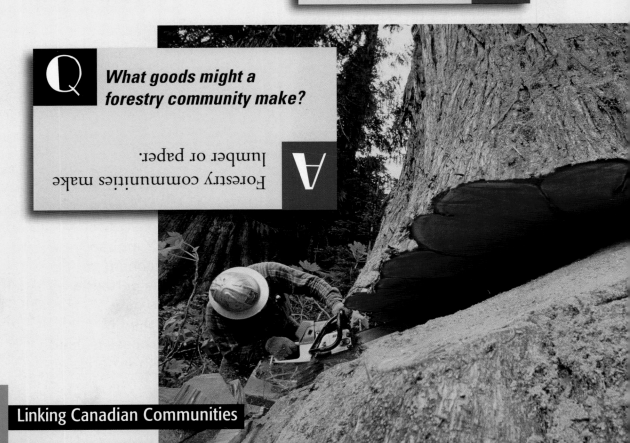

Q **What is the difference between a rural and urban community?**

A A rural community has plenty of open space and few people. An urban community has taller buildings and more people.

Q **How do pulp and paper mills harm the environment?**

A They release chemicals into the air and water.

Q **Where are forestry communities usually found?**

A They are usually found near forests.

Making Paper

Materials

- used paper (newspaper, wrapping paper)
- a large bowl filled with water
- a wire mesh sheet
- a plastic bag
- books or other heavy objects

Procedure

1. Tear the paper into small pieces, and let it soak overnight in the bowl of water.
2. The next day, mash the soaked paper into a pulp with your hands.
3. Outdoors or in a bathtub, pour the bucket of paper pulp over the wire mesh sheet.
4. Spread the pulp out evenly with your hands, and push down, squeezing out the extra water.
5. Place a plastic bag on top of the pulp, and weigh it down with books or other heavy objects.
6. Leave the pulp to dry for a few hours.
7. Remove the books and plastic, and gently peel the paper from the mesh. Allow the pieces to dry on a flat surface. Now, you have made paper.

Further Research

Many books and websites provide information on forestry communities. To learn more about forestry communities, borrow books from the library, or surf the Internet.

Books

Most libraries have computers that connect to a database for researching information. If you input a key word, you will be provided with a list of books in the library that contain information on that topic. Non-fiction books are arranged numerically, using their call number. Fiction books are organized alphabetically by the author's last name.

Websites

The World Wide Web is also a good source of information. Reliable websites often include government sites, educational sites, and online encyclopedias. Type in key search terms, such as "logging," "trees," and "pulp mills," into the search engine to learn more about these topics.

To learn more about Powell River, visit Powell River's tourism website. **www.discoverpowellriver.com**

To find out more about the paper-making process and how to reduce paper waste, visit the Energy Kid's Page, and type "paper" into the search field. **www.eia.doe.gov/kids**

To read about British Columbia's forests and forestry industry, go to BC Forest Information. **www.bcforestinformation.com**

Words to Know

bleached: made white

grade: to sort by level of quality

hectares: areas containing 10,000 square metres

legal: not against the law

lumber: wooden boards for building

manufacturing: making a large amount of something using machines

minerals: inorganic substances that are obtained through mining

natural resources: materials found in nature, such as water, soil, and forests, that can be used by people

oxygen: a gas that makes up one fifth of the air

peroxide: a chemical used in the bleaching of paper

timber: logs before they are cut into wooden boards for building

Index